HAMMERHEAD SHARKS

HAMMERHEAD SHARKS

By Joyce A. Hull

MASON CREST

Mason Crest
450 Parkway Drive, Suite D
Broomall, Pennsylvania 19008
(866) MCP-BOOK (toll-free)
www.masoncrest.com

First printing
9 8 7 6 5 4 3 2 1
Printed in the USA

ISBN (hardback) 978-1-4222-4127-1
ISBN (series) 978-1-4222-4121-9
ISBN (ebook) 978-1-4222-7676-1

Library of Congress Cataloging-in-Publication Data

Names: Hull, Joyce A., author.
Title: Hammerhead sharks / Joyce A. Hull.
Description: Broomall, Pennsylvania: Mason Crest, [2019] | Series: The amazing world of sharks | Includes bibliographical references and index.
Identifiers: LCCN 2018013890 (print) | LCCN 2018019034 (ebook) | ISBN 9781422276761 (eBook) | ISBN 9781422241271 (hardback) | ISBN 9781422241219 (series)
Subjects: LCSH: Hammerhead sharks--Juvenile literature.
Classification: LCC QL638.95.S7 (ebook) | LCC QL638.95.S7 H85 2019 (print) | DDC 597.3/4--dc23
LC record available at https://lccn.loc.gov/2018013890

Developed and Produced by National Highlights Inc.
Editors: Keri De Deo and Mika Jin
Interior and cover design: Priceless Digital Media
Production: Michelle Luke

CONTENTS

KEY ICONS TO LOOK FOR:

Words to Understand: These words with their easy-to-understand definitions will increase the reader's understanding of the text while building vocabulary skills.

Sidebars: This boxed material within the main text allows readers to build knowledge, gain insights, explore possibilities, and broaden their perspectives by weaving together additional information to provide realistic and holistic perspectives.

Educational Videos: Readers can view videos by scanning our QR codes, providing them with additional educational content to supplement the text. Examples include news coverage, moments in history, speeches, iconic sports moments, and much more!

Text-Dependent Questions: These questions send the reader back to the text for more careful attention to the evidence presented there.

Research Projects: Readers are pointed toward areas of further inquiry connected to each chapter. Suggestions are provided for projects that encourage deeper research and analysis.

Series Glossary of Key Terms: This back-of-the book glossary contains terminology used throughout this series. Words found here increase the reader's ability to read and comprehend higher-level books and articles in this field.

FUN FACTS...
GETTING TO KNOW THEM

TIGER SHARK
Named for the vertical striped markings along its body, but they fade with age.

MAKO SHARK
Known as the race car of sharks for its fast swimming speed!

BULL SHARK
Named for its stocky shape, broad, flat snout, and aggressive, unpredictable behavior!

RAYS
Rays and sharks belong to the same family. A ray is basically a flattened shark.

GREAT WHITE SHARK
With jaws this fierce, they don't call it "Great" for nothing!

BLUE SHARK
Known by their distinct blue and white coloring, their large eyes, and long snout.

HAMMERHEAD SHARK
Yes, those are eyes mounted on the side of its head, giving it 360-degree vision!

THRESHER SHARK
This clever shark uses its unique long tail fin to stun and catch prey!

WORDS TO UNDERSTAND:

ampulla: A long groove that has two bulb-shaped globes at the end.

electroreception: Detecting the electrical impulses given off by living things.

symbiotic: A relationship between two species that is beneficial to both.

viviparous: Giving birth to a live, fully-formed baby.

CHAPTER 1

INTRODUCING HAMMERHEAD SHARKS

NICE TAN!

Hammerhead sharks are one of the few species of animals that get a tan from the sun. This happens when they spend time in shallow waters, which is where they most like spending time.

Although hammerhead sharks eat a variety of fish, they won't eat angelfish.

SHARK WASH

Hammerhead sharks and king angelfish have a **symbiotic** relationship. Hammerheads visit "cleaning stations" manned by king angelfish. At these locations, the angelfish eat any parasites and clean the shark. In return for their services, hammerheads won't eat king angelfish.

HAMMERHEAD MYTHS

Native Hawaiians call the hammerhead *mano kihikihi*. They respect all sharks and believe they are the returned spirits of dead loved ones. The hammerhead isn't seen often in this area, but when it is, the Hawaiians believe it is a special protector (*aumakua*). When a child is born with the hammerhead as its spirit animal, these natives believe that the child is to become a great sea warrior.

Hammerhead sharks are some of the most recognizable members of the shark family because of the unusual shape of their heads. Their heads are distinguished by a large horizontal extension with an eye located at each end. The nostrils rest across the front of this hammer-like structure, and a mouth full of razor-sharp teeth sits beneath. The hammerhead's mouth is smaller than that

Watch hammerheads in action as they hunt!

The hammerhead shark is one of the most recognizable shark species around.

of other shark species, and hunting is easier when they seek out prey along the bottom of the ocean. Nature has helped make this hunting preference easier by providing an off-white belly that helps disguise the hammerhead when viewed from underneath. The upper coloring is gray-brown, sometimes olive green.

WIDE VARIETY

Scientists currently have discovered ten different kinds of hammerhead sharks. Hammerheads live between twenty and thirty years. They all share the distinctive hammer-shaped nose, but each species has a slightly different design to this hammer. The smallest hammerheads are only 3 ft. (.9144 m) long and weigh less than 7 lbs. (3.18 kg). The largest, the great hammerhead, can grow up to 20 ft. (6.096 m) in length and weigh as much as 1,200 lbs. (544.3108 kg). This variety in size makes it difficult to create general statements about this species because each has special traits that set it apart from the rest. Like humans, however, there are some traits that are shared by all.

Hammerhead sharks are extremely agile.

HOW THE HAMMER HELPS

Scientists have tried to figure out why the hammerhead has such a unique nose. It has been difficult because this shark, like all sharks, has an internal structure that is made up mainly of cartilage instead of bone. When any part of an ancient hammerhead has been found, it has been mainly teeth. Theories have included the idea that the nose structure evolved to help with seeing. Other theories suggest that the special design of the hammerhead's nose helps the species smell its prey. However, scientists have finally decided that the shape of the head, while helping with sight and smell, is more helpful with movement.

The lack of bone within the hammerhead makes it easier for them to turn quickly when hunting or avoiding an attack. Their skeletons are made of cartilage, similar to the composition of the human ear. This allows it to bend freely. Scientists have noted that the hammerhead can tilt its nose in a way that the water lifts its nose, creating momentum when the shark turns. Think of the ends of the hammer like the wings of an airplane. By tilting the plane's wings slightly, the air helps the plane turn easier. This is how the nose of the hammerhead works.

SIDEBAR

BABY HAMMERHEADS

Hammerheads are **viviparous** animals which means they give birth to a live, fully-formed baby. The babies, then, are born looking like their adult counterparts. Female hammerheads produce eggs like humans do. The male fertilizes the eggs while they are inside the female, and she then remains pregnant for seven months. Females give birth to between six and fifty babies, called pups, each year. This number is dependent upon the size and weight of the mother. Smaller members of the species give birth to a larger number of pups. When the babies are born, they huddle together for warmth and protection until they are strong enough to go out on their own. Hammerheads don't make good parents as they don't stay with the pups once they are born, and the young ones must survive on their own.

Baby hammerhead sharks look just like their parents.

GENTLE CREATURES

Of the ten known types of hammerheads, only three have ever been known to attack humans. These are the great, the scalloped, and the smooth hammerheads. Even these sharks have never been known to attack someone unprovoked, and there have been no known deaths associated with these attacks. Much like a dog, a hammerhead will only bite when it is feeling threatened, and only enough to get away. Divers have spent hours swimming peacefully with several species of hammerhead sharks. Most members of the hammerhead species wiggle and twist as a warning that they are feeling threatened. If this warning dance is heeded, and a swimmer backs off, the hammerhead continues on its way without attacking.

Hammerhead sharks like to hang out in large groups.

THE WORLD OF THE HAMMERHEAD

Hammerheads spend most of their time in warm waters, but they will migrate to cooler water when the temperature becomes too hot. Get ready to explore the daily world of the hammerhead!

HUNTING

Hammerheads differ from other shark species in that they can be found hunting in schools of up to a hundred during the day. At night, they return to hunting alone. This is when they seek out their favorite meal, the stingray. Hammerheads have special organs called the **ampullae** of Lorenzini. These organs enhance **electroreception**, which is the hammerhead's main hunting tool.

All living things send out electrical impulses. The hammerhead can detect these electrical signals and find where their prey is hiding. Rays hide under the sandy bottom of the sea, as do many of the other regular meals of the hammerhead. By honing in on the electrical impulses with its ampullae, the hammerhead can find its prey. The hammerhead will then hold down the ray with its nose and enjoy the meal.

This ability to sense electrical impulses is important for the hammerhead because it has a blind spot directly in front of it. The location of its eyes on the sides of its skull makes it possible for the hammerhead to see easily both above and below it, but looking directly ahead is impossible. With such a small mouth located beneath this extension, using electrical impulses to find prey hiding beneath the sand is perfect.

TEXT-DEPENDENT QUESTIONS:

1. What is the favorite food of hammerhead sharks, and how do they hunt for this prey?
2. Why has it been difficult for scientists to discover the actual evolutionary process of the hammerhead?
3. Discuss one unusual hunting habit of the hammerhead that is rarely seen in other sharks.

RESEARCH PROJECT:

Visit https://www.thoughtco.com/hammerhead-sharks-2291435 and read about the ten different types of hammerhead sharks. When you find the one that has been newly discovered, look for information on how it was discovered and write a one-page paper with the details.

WORDS TO UNDERSTAND:

apex predator: A predator that is at the top of the food chain and does not have a natural enemy that regularly hunts it.

estuaries: Places where river water and ocean water meet.

pelagic zone: The open ocean—the area that is not near the bottom of the ocean or close to shore.

submarine volcano: A volcano that is located completely under the sea.

temperate: Denotes a warm climate that isn't as hot as tropical weather.

CHAPTER 2

THE HAMMERHEAD'S POPULATION AND HABITAT

VACATIONS

Everyone needs a vacation! Like many animals, hammerheads typically migrate to a different climate during the hottest times of the year. During summer, large schools of hammerhead sharks will gather and head away from the equator. It is during this time of year that people in the New England area of the United

The Solomon Islands, off the coast of Australia, are a favorite "vacation" spot for hammerhead sharks.

States are more likely to see a hammerhead visiting their beaches or swimming alongside a boat. One reason for this migration is that the hammerhead is susceptible to sunburn. The hammerheads can't tolerate water that is too warm. You can't blame them! You wouldn't want to swim in hot water either!

SIDEBAR

SHARKANO

Scientists haven't explored the waters around the Solomon Islands very much because it is some of the deepest water in the ocean and difficult to reach. Despite this, a group of researchers ventured into this area to see what they could discover within the **submarine volcano** named Kavachi. They expected to discover interesting rocks and maybe some plant life, but they discovered much more. At first, their camera found some small fish and some jellyfish. The scientists were pleasantly surprised, but suddenly, a large number of hammerhead sharks appeared. All of these creatures seemed comfortably at home, until they noticed the camera. Seeing the camera as a threat, these sharks tried to attack it. Imagine how stunned, and thrilled, the scientists were when they reviewed the film and discovered the hammerheads! The scientists are anxious to study this active volcano further because they were shocked to see that the sea life living inside it was not bothered by the volcano at all. This is one more example of how little we know about the deep ocean and the beings that call it home.

This video shows hammerheads and other sea life living inside the underwater volcano near Solomon Island.

Hammerhead sharks can be found in areas of the ocean where the water is either tropical or **temperate**. All hammerhead species, except the great hammerhead, prefer shallow waters. Because of its large size, the great hammerhead prefers deep ocean water and is often found in places frequented by whales.

Living in shallow water has both good and bad consequences. On one hand, it makes it easier for hammerhead sharks to enjoy their favorite foods, which are often found on the ocean floor. On the other hand, it makes hammerheads more vulnerable to being hunted by humans. This last point is why the population of these sharks is decreasing.

Different species of hammerhead sharks can be found in different areas. However, most hammerheads spend their time in what is known as the **pelagic zone** around large land masses, and near reefs where plenty of food can be found. Reefs also provide natural protection from humans. Although hammerhead sharks prefer living near reefs, they can be found in **estuaries**, sandy plains, and kelp forests, too.

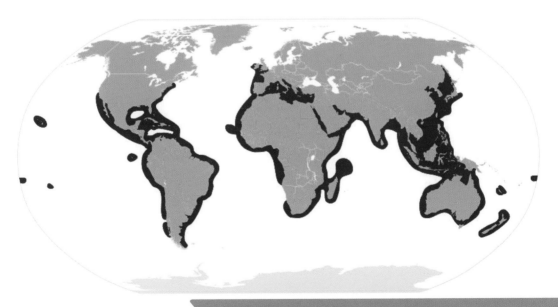

Most hammerhead sharks prefer to stick to coastal waters.

If you want to find a particular species of hammerhead, it helps to know the areas of the world they are most likely to enjoy. Some types of hammerheads can be found in many places, and others live only in a small area. For example, in the case of the Carolina hammerhead, which has only recently been discovered, biologists don't know enough about it to know where it lives other than the South Carolina coast. As they learn more, they may find it living in other areas. They might also have to change its name!

Here is where you can find each of the other nine types of hammerhead sharks:

Great Hammerhead – The largest member of the hammerhead family has been found in the Atlantic, Pacific, and Indian Oceans. Some great hammerheads have also been found living in the Mediterranean and Black Seas and the Arabian Gulf.

Smooth Hammerhead – These sharks have been found in a variety of places, including the freshwater of Florida's Indian River. In the United States, look along the western coastline of California and the waters around Hawaii. Other places to find the smooth hammerhead are in Australia, South America, Europe, and Africa.

Scalloped Hammerhead – This hammerhead species has been studied the most and has been found in the greatest number of places. It likes to live close to shores and has been found off the coast of New Jersey and Uruguay. A large population also lives in the Pacific Ocean near Southern California and off the shores of Hawaii. Scalloped hammerheads have also been found living in the Red Sea, Indian Ocean, and the western Pacific from Japan to Australia.

Scalloped Bonnethead – This shark is the only one of the hammerheads that prefers living near fresh water. It can be found swimming around in shallow bays and estuaries. The western Atlantic from South Carolina

The scalloped hammerhead is just one of many kinds of hammerhead sharks.

to Brazil and the eastern Pacific from California to Ecuador contain many scalloped bonnetheads, as do the Caribbean and the Gulf of Mexico.

Winghead – Members of this group of hammerheads are most often found in the Indo-West Pacific from the Persian Gulf to the Philippines and from China to Australia.

Hammerheads dig for their prey under the sand.

Scoophead – The scoophead calls both the Atlantic and the Pacific Oceans home. Look for it from the Gulf of California to Peru in the eastern Pacific and from Panama to Brazil in the western Atlantic.

Bonnethead – The bonnethead lives in estuaries and shallow bays in subtropical waters of both the Atlantic and Pacific. They can be found from South Carolina to Brazil in the Atlantic and from California to Ecuador in the Pacific.

Smalleye and Whitefin – So far, the smalleye and whitefin hammerheads exist in a limited area. The smalleye seems to prefer the eastern coast of South America, and the whitefin can be found in the eastern Atlantic off the coast of Africa.

GOING WHERE THE FOOD GOES

Hammerheads often hunt for prey along the ocean floor. The unique shape of their noses causes the hammerhead to have a smaller mouth than most other sharks. Its mouth is also positioned more toward the underside of its head because of the nose shape. It is much easier for the hammerhead to travel across the ocean floor and locate food that is buried beneath the sand. This is especially helpful when they seek out stingrays, their favorite food.

Stingrays try to protect themselves by hiding under the sand. The hammerhead is able to cruise along the ocean floor and use its electrolocation skills to sniff out the rays. It then pins the ray down with its nose and is in a position to eat without having to loosen its grip on the meal. Most sea life is hurt by the sting of the rays, but hammerheads appear to be immune to the ray's sting. Crabs, another favorite food, also make their home on the ocean bottom.

Hammerhead sharks have few predators.

BIRTHING ENVIRONMENT

We learned earlier that hammerheads make bad parents. When giving birth, the mother hammerhead swims even closer to shore than normal. Once born, the pups are forced to survive on their own until they become adults. To stay safe, the pups stay in shallow water and stick together to offer each other protection.

This means pups can be found near shore where their food is smaller and easier for them to catch. People who see a group of hammerhead sharks in shallow water can guess that they are babies. If left alone, the baby hammerheads will gladly remain where they can find food. If they were to be born out in deeper waters, they would not survive because they are so small and unskilled. It is possible that this early need to form a school for protection is what created the hammerhead's tendency to gather in schools once they reach adulthood.

As you wander farther away from shore, the deeper the water becomes and the larger the fish are. This is why hammerheads do not venture far from shore. Other than the great hammerhead, most hammerhead sharks dive only a distance of 98.5 ft. (30 m) down. Most hammerheads do not grow large enough to stay safe in these deeper waters. If one of the smaller types does happen to find its way into these regions, it becomes food for fish that are both larger and stronger.

Like most sharks, hammerheads are considered apex predators. In their natural area, hammerheads are normally at the top of the food chain. This does not mean, however, that they are never eaten by some other predator. Baby hammerheads, for example, are at risk from larger sea animals because they are small and vulnerable. Larger hammerheads may also eat smaller ones if they are hungry and no other food is nearby. In nature, animals that are injured or ill become targets for other animals, sometimes even of their own species. This is true for hammerheads as well. Normally, however, hammerhead sharks do not have to worry about any predators except humans.

FINDING THE HAMMERHEAD

Two of the most popular places to find hammerheads are near an uninhabited island named Cocos Island and near the Galapagos Islands. Cocos Island is located about 340 mi. (547 km) off the coast of Costa Rica. The Galapagos are about 600 mi. (966 km) west of Ecuador. These two places offer the hammerhead a perfect environment. The waters are warm without being too hot, and they are shallower than other areas of the ocean. In the case of Cocos Island, there are no people on the island except special rangers who are given the task of preserving life on and around the island. This means the hammerhead is not likely to find itself, or its food supply, becoming dinner for humans. More of the babies survive, which helps to increase the population. Because the hammerhead is in danger of becoming extinct, the greater the number of pups that survive, the better off the species becomes.

Having both quantity and variety of food choices in these areas, the hammerhead is able to hunt regularly and does not have to wander too far from safety to find dinner. Because fishermen are not near these locations, the hammerhead can be assured of finding enough food and is not in danger of being hunted or accidentally harmed by being caught in fishing nets.

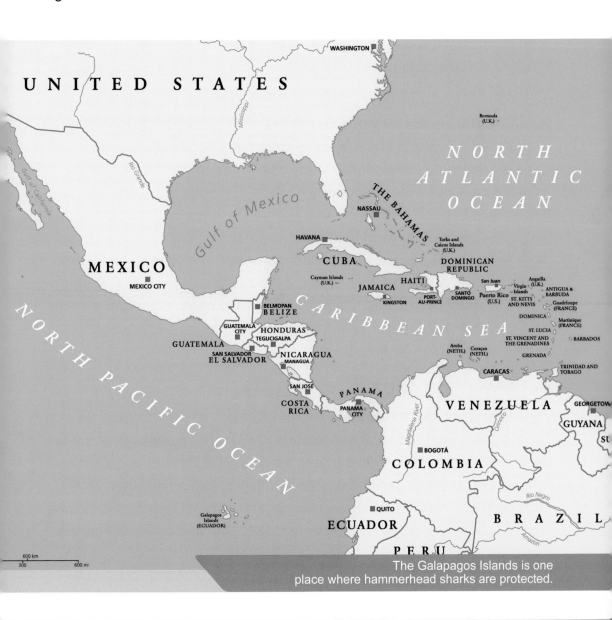

The Galapagos Islands is one place where hammerhead sharks are protected.

COCOS ISLAND

Cocos Island stays at a fairly even temperature of 79°F (26.1°C) year round. This means that the coral reef where hammerheads live is located in water that remains at a fairly constant temperature. The water is neither too shallow nor too deep. The water not only has the coral reef, but it also has tunnels and caves that give the sea creatures that live there plenty of places to hide. It makes sense that divers have found this area to be the home of sixty species of crustaceans, six hundred species of mollusks, and over three hundred species of fish. The crustaceans alone give the hammerhead a variety of food choices.

Human visitors to the island must get permission from the park rangers who protect it. Visitors are subject to strict rules as to how long they can stay and what they can do. Many divers find this the ideal place for adventure because they can easily observe the huge variety of life that takes place beneath the water. The marine life is not bothered by fishermen, and the rather safe environment creates an atmosphere of trust. Divers are more likely to get a close view of hammerheads in a stress-free environment for the sharks. All divers have to leave the island at night and find other places to sleep because they are not allowed to camp overnight. It is not hard to imagine that if all hammerheads could, they would choose this perfect environment as home.

GALAPAGOS ISLANDS

The Galapagos are actually a group of islands: eighteen large ones and three smaller ones. In all, these islands house approximately twenty-five thousand people. This makes it very friendly for both land and sea life. The area is protected, so there is no hunting or fishing allowed. This protection has made it a place where safety is something the non-human life has come to expect. This security makes the land and sea animals friendlier.

Many sharks, like this scalloped hammerhead, are threatened species.

Water temperatures stay fairly consistent throughout the year and range from 72°F to 76°F (about 22°C to 24°C). Divers are allowed to go beneath the water in a limited number of areas throughout the islands. The groups are required to stay small, and time limits of two to four hours are enforced. These regulations help keep the sea life feeling less stressed because it is not constantly being subjected to human contact. This area doesn't offer the variety of hiding spots that Cocos Island offers, and the regular volcanic activity makes the undersea environment rockier.

Hammerhead populations are decreasing in this area, however. Illegal fishing is becoming a problem. Also, in 2001, an oil tanker became stranded and created an oil spill that affected hammerheads and much of the sea life. Hammerhead sharks had been leaving the area, but in recent years they have been returning as the effects of the oil spill dissipate.

FEWER SAFE PLACES

What's happening in the Galapagos is an example of how the hammerhead shark is losing some of its long-time living environments. Many countries now make it illegal to actively hunt sharks, but that doesn't stop illegal hunters from killing sharks when they get the chance. One of the reasons hammerheads are killed, especially the great hammerhead, is because in many places of the world shark fin soup is considered something special. It is especially sad that many fishermen will catch a shark and cut off its fins while it is still alive. They then throw the shark back into the water where it can't swim properly and will quickly die. Even when fishermen don't try to catch shark, many are caught in fishing nets where they become stuck and die.

In some parts of the world, the hammerhead is losing living space due to coastal development. As humans take over the land close to shore, they make it difficult for the shark to find its normal food. The hammerhead is also bothered by humans who believe they are in danger of being attacked by sharks. Humans will try to force the hammerheads living close to shore to become so stressed that they move away from the land. Because of this, mother hammerheads can't always find a suitable place to give birth in areas that sharks have been doing so for generations.

Now that we have seen where the hammerhead enjoys living, it is time to explore how the body of the hammerhead helps it survive in these environments.

TEXT-DEPENDENT QUESTIONS:

1. While hammerheads enjoy eating stingrays most, what second favorite food is available in Cocos Island?

2. What are the two main reasons hammerheads prefer shallow water?

3. Thinking about the areas hammerheads enjoy living the most, what is the ideal water temperature for these sharks?

RESEARCH PROJECT:

Each habitat has its own food chain. A shark living in deep water will see a different food chain than one living in shallow water. Pick out one of the favorite habitats of the hammerhead shark and create a poster that shows the natural food chain for the hammerhead. What things would change if the hammerhead lived in one of the Great Lakes?

WORDS TO UNDERSTAND:

dorsal: Located on the top or back of something.

placoid scales: Scales made of tooth-like enamel that cover the skin of the shark. They are also known as dermal denticles.

ram ventilation: The process of removing oxygen from seawater that passes through a fish's mouth and out through the gills.

CHAPTER 3

THE HAMMERHEAD'S DIET, BEHAVIOR, AND BIOLOGY

THAT'S A MOUTHFUL

Can you imagine growing as many as thirty thousand teeth in your lifetime? That is exactly how many teeth scientists believe an average shark grows. A shark is constantly losing teeth. Sometimes it is a matter of a tooth getting broken accidentally, but normally a tooth will reach a certain age and fall out. Most sharks have several rows of teeth. As one tooth falls out, the tooth behind it moves forward to take its place. A new tooth then grows behind it. This process goes on throughout the entire life of the shark. This is why it's not unusual to find shark teeth washed up on the beach.

The skull of this hammerhead shows its unique structure.

SIDEBAR

DOLPHIN OR SHARK?

You're swimming in the ocean and see a **dorsal** fin sticking up above the water. Is it a shark or a dolphin heading your way? It is easy to tell the difference between the two if you know what to look for. The dorsal fin of a shark has a straight edge on the rear side. The dolphin's fin, on the other hand, curves back towards its tail. Knowing this difference can also alert you to the shark's direction. If the straight edge is closest to you, he is just passing by and heading away.

Just how did the hammerhead develop its hammer?

Hammerhead sharks have a biological design that makes them perfect for life in the ocean. Each part of its body serves a unique purpose and works together to create a finely-tuned creature that is wonderful to behold. Hammerheads have a diet that is varied and helps them adapt to the many different environments where they find themselves. Their habits differ from other shark species in certain ways, making them unique in more than just appearance. These habits can, however, make them more susceptible to danger than other types of sharks. Let's take a look at how nature designed the hammerhead.

THE HAMMERHEAD'S SENSES

The first thing you notice about the hammerhead is the shape of its nose, which is how it got its name. These sharks, of which there are ten different types, have noses that look like a hammer. The nose has an eye situated at each end, and the front of the nose is rimmed with sensory organs that allow the hammerhead to smell and to sense electrical impulses from moving objects in its environment. The placement of its eyes allows the hammerhead to be able to see above and below it at the same time. This works great when it is trying to stay safe while swimming.

One problem with the position of its eyes is that the hammerhead has a blind spot, which is directly in front of it. With its ability to feel electrical impulses, however, the shark can turn quickly when it senses something in this spot. Internal ears also aid in detecting vibrations from the movement of objects in its surroundings. Despite this blind spot, hammerheads have excellent vision compared to many ocean dwellers. The pupils of their eyes dilate and contract, meaning they get larger and smaller, depending on how much light is available. Inside the eye, the hammerhead's

retina picks up light sources. The light is then directed behind the retina where there is a layer called the tapetum lucidum. This layer is made up of a silver crystal material that reflects the light. This allows the hammerhead to see in lower light levels. To protect the eye from injury, a thin membrane closes whenever the shark is eating or when something gets close to its eye.

The design of the hammerhead makes them excellent hunters.

The large area covered by the hammerhead's nose and its ability to sense movement aid it well during hunting. Its nose is so sensitive that it can detect blood among all the other smells in the ocean, and this sends it in the right direction towards food. The hammerhead likes to search for food on the ocean floor whenever possible. Its mouth is further down than the mouths of other sharks because of the wide nose. This makes it more difficult to feed on prey that is swimming at or above nose level. The nose design also gives the hammerhead a smaller mouth than other breeds of shark. Its favorite meal is the stingray. The ray hides beneath the sand on the ocean's floor, but the hammerhead has no problem locating it. When the shark finds a ray, it holds the ray down with its flat nose while its mouth is in the perfect position to eat the stingray.

You may wonder if a hammerhead can actually taste what it eats. This is one area that scientists have not studied well. It isn't like they can ask the shark if it enjoyed its meal. Scientists believe the hammerhead does have some form of taste buds, however, because the hammerhead has been observed spitting out certain foods. This is a subject that needs further study. For now, it is not known whether sharks eat a particular prey because it is easier to catch or if it tastes better than other prey.

SKIN

Hammerheads have skin that appears smooth, but it feels like sandpaper to the touch. The hammerhead's skin contains teeth-shaped scales called **placoid scales**, or dermal denticles. These scales form a type of mesh that attaches to the muscles and creates a kind of armor for the hammerhead. This protects it when needed because the scales resemble sharp teeth that cut an attacker. With most fish, you can use the rows of scales to figure out how long the fish has lived. You can't do this with the hammerhead, however. These outer scales don't grow as it does, and they stop growing after the shark reaches a certain size.

The coloring of the hammerhead makes it hard to see in the ocean.

The coloring of the hammerhead serves as camouflage for hunting. The upper side of the shark is a brownish-green color that blends in with the surrounding sea when seen from above. Creatures below the hammerhead see an off-white belly that blends in with the sea's surface. No matter which side of a hammerhead a fish views, all it sees is a slightly darker shape that blends in well with the surrounding water.

FINS

Fins are the most familiar part of any shark. These are the triangular-shaped attachments and the tail. These fins are what enable the hammerhead to swim swiftly and straight. They also help him turn quickly without flipping sideways. On males, there is also a fin that aids in reproduction. These are the five fins:

a. **Pectoral** – These fins are located underneath the hammerhead in the chest area. The pectoral fins help the hammerhead steer and allow it to lift itself upward as it moves toward higher areas.

b. **Pelvic** – These fins are located underneath the shark and more towards its tail. The purpose for these fins is mainly to keep the hammerhead from going off balance. In male hammerheads, the pelvic fins are used to grasp the female so the two can mate.

c. **Dorsal** – This is the fin you are most familiar with. It is located behind the shark's head on its back. This large fin creates stability for the hammerhead, allowing it to remain upright. It also tells humans when the hammerhead is close to the water's surface as it is the first part of the hammerhead to become visible on top of the water.

d. **Anal** – These small fins are located underneath the hammerhead near its tail. Their purpose is also to help stabilize the shark as it moves.

e. **Caudal** – This is the hammerhead's tail. The caudal fin is divided into two sections above and below the body. It aids the hammerhead's forward movement through the water.

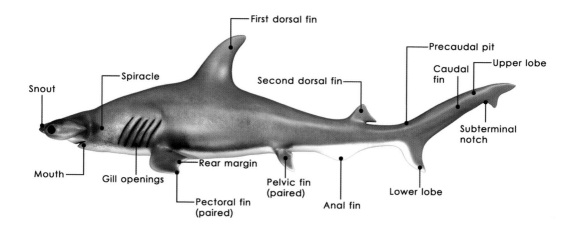

Diagram of a hammerhead shark

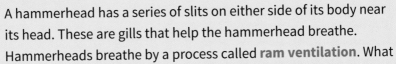

BREATHING

A hammerhead has a series of slits on either side of its body near its head. These are gills that help the hammerhead breathe.

Hammerheads breathe by a process called **ram ventilation**. What occurs during this process is that as the hammerhead moves forward, water passes through the mouth and out the gills. Inside the gills, specialized blood vessels draw oxygen from the water. The oxygen is then transported through the blood vessels to other parts of the body, much like in humans. The unused hydrogen from the water continues through the gills and is released back into the ocean.

Some fish, including a few species of shark, have an extra part near the gills that draws water into the shark when it is still. The hammerhead does not have this body part and must keep moving at all times to keep water flowing past the gills. This means that hammerheads are moving even when they are asleep. If they remain still for more than a few seconds, they will basically suffocate.

INTERNAL ORGANS

Inside the hammerhead are many of the same organs that humans have, although they may not perform the same function. The internal organs include a heart, stomach, spleen, pancreas, rectum, liver, and brain. The heart, brain, and liver are fascinating.

The hammerhead's heart is made up of only two chambers, called the atrium and the ventricle. This is located in the head region of the shark. One chamber takes oxygenated blood from the gills and sends it throughout the shark's body. The other chamber receives deoxygenated blood that is returning from the shark's body. The blood is sent back to the gills, where the cycle begins again.

The largest internal organ of the hammerhead is its liver. The liver is so large it accounts for 25 percent of the hammerhead's body weight. The liver serves two very important functions. First, it is here that fat is stored. This fat is used for energy by the shark. The second purpose of the liver is to keep the hammerhead from sinking. The oils that make up the fat in its liver weigh less than the surrounding ocean water. This allows the shark to stay afloat instead of sinking to the bottom of the sea.

The brain inside a hammerhead is larger than that of many other sharks. This allows the hammerhead to develop certain skills that other sharks do not exhibit. Some biologists currently study how much this allows the hammerhead to think better. They do believe that certain behaviors that differ in this shark are a result of its larger brain. While its larger brain puts the hammerhead among the smartest of sharks, it may also be responsible for one of the behaviors that puts the hammerhead at risk, which is gathering in schools. We'll take a look at that after discussing the life cycle.

SIDEBAR

DAILY LIFE

Unlike most shark species, who spend their lives swimming alone all the time, hammerheads have a tendency to gather in large groups called schools during the day. Amazingly, the sharks have developed a way to communicate with each other using body language. It is not known exactly why they gather in schools, but many scientists believe it is a way to protect themselves from larger predators in the ocean. This can be beneficial when the hammerhead must migrate to cooler waters in the summer. What is even more amazing is that these schools aren't simply a group of random hammerheads gathering in the same area. Each school has an internal structure that is socially organized and gives status to individuals based on size, age, and gender. You could almost look at these schools as similar to a family. Unlike a family, however, the hammerheads go their separate ways at night to hunt alone.

It is this schooling behavior that is risky for the hammerhead. While it is believed that they gather as a way to be protected, this very behavior makes them a target for shark hunters who will go where the schools form to get the greatest number of sharks in as little time as possible.

Although hammerhead sharks prefer stingrays, they'll eat all kinds of fish such as this Caribbean Reef Squid.

THE HAMMERHEAD'S LIFE CYCLE

Hammerhead sharks live an average of twenty-five to thirty-five years. They are unlike many fish in that they do not lay eggs but give birth to live offspring, called pups. A male hammerhead impregnates a female, and she remains pregnant for seven months. During that time, the babies are given nourishment through a yolk sac that is attached to the baby and the mother. This is almost identical to the way humans nourish their young while pregnant. When it is time for the pups to be born, mother hammerheads swim to shallow water, and the pups are born alive and ready to try to survive on their own. The pups are only 20 – 28 in. (50.8 cm – 71.12 cm) long when they are first born.

After giving birth, the mother shark swims back into deeper water. Her pups are left behind to fend for themselves. The pups feed on small bony fish and crabs. They stick together for protection until each one is large enough to survive on its own. The female hammerhead is considered mature when she is 8 – 10 ft. (2.44 m – 3.048 m) long. The male is smaller at maturity. He is between 7 and 9 ft. (2.1336 m – 2.7432 m) long.

Mature hammerheads enjoy a wide variety of food. We've already talked about how their favorite dinner is the stingray, but hammerheads also enjoy shrimp, squid, crab, herring, toadfish, grouper, tarpon, sardines, boxfish, and sea catfish. Notice that humans are not part of the hammerhead's diet. They tend to taste funny and not be fatty enough for the hammerhead's taste. When its normal diet isn't available, hammerheads may even eat smaller sharks. This wide variety of food choices allows the hammerhead to find food in almost any area in which it finds itself. Hunting takes place twice a day, at dusk and at dawn.

TEXT-DEPENDENT QUESTIONS:

1. How does the hammerhead's heart differ from that of a human?

2. Describe how the hammerhead shark breathes.

3. Why is it both helpful and harmful for hammerheads to travel in schools?

 RESEARCH PROJECT:

Collect a chopstick and a straw wrapper of the same length. The chopstick represents a fish that has a bony skeleton and the straw wrapper represents a hammerhead with cartilage instead of bones. Using cardboard, create a maze that has at least three ninety-degree turns. Make the width of the path only 2 in. (5.08 cm) wide. First, have the straw wrapper "swim" through the maze. Now do the same with the chopstick. What happens? How would the hammerhead be hindered if it had a bony skeleton?

WORDS TO UNDERSTAND:

bycatch: When fishermen seek to catch one kind of fish, usually in a net or a cage, but a different kind of marine animal is caught too.

docile: Something or someone that is calm or gentle.

excursion: A vacation that is often led by a guide and includes adventure.

CHAPTER 4

ENCOUNTERING A HAMMERHEAD SHARK

PEOPLE BITES

Sharks often have a reputation for being vicious, but this isn't always the case. Some scientists actually calculate the number of shark bites and compare them to bites from other species. These studies show that you are more likely to be bitten by a human being in New York City than bitten by a shark in the ocean. Imagine a human being actually taking a bite out of you!

Studying hammerhead sharks can help save them.

SIDEBAR

HUMANS TASTE NASTY

Among sharks, hammerheads are the least likely to attack a human being. Like all sharks, hammerheads do not eat humans. An attack from a shark normally occurs because the shark feels threatened and cannot escape. When they do attack, a simple bite is all they often resort to. Much like a cat, they bite to escape a situation. Sharks will swim away as soon as possible in most cases. On the rare occasion a shark does attack, death normally occurs from loss of blood or because the shark's teeth punctured an important organ, not because a shark consumed the person. Sharks may not consider humans friends, but they also do not consider them food.

Tracking sharks (The video is at the top of the article.)

Hammerhead sharks aren't something you come across every day, especially if you live nowhere near an ocean. This does not mean you have to go your entire life without coming into contact with a hammerhead. Seeing one of these incredible creatures in person is something you will remember for the rest of your life. Different people have different opinions on how close they

People can safely dive with hammerhead sharks in the Bahamas.

would like to be to a hammerhead. Some wish for the chance to actually swim with these sharks. Others would be happy to simply see videos that bring them closer. Let's explore some of the safe ways you can learn more about the hammerhead.

DIVING EXCURSIONS

Joining a group of other people who want to get eye-to-eye with hammerheads can be a great way to see these sharks. To join an **excursion**, first do some research into where hammerheads gather, and then look for companies that offer diving adventures. The best places are those where the hammerhead population hasn't been reduced because of **bycatch**. This research is important since many places have experienced a decline in hammerhead population. It would be a shame to spend all that money to see a hammerhead, and then not get to see one. Although one of the costliest ways to get close to a hammerhead, diving excursions provide one of the most unforgettable ways, too!

Most ocean islands that have a large population of hammerheads offer guided tours. These can be done one of three different ways: by boat, cage diving, or free diving. Some people prefer to stay in the safety of a boat and see the sharks swim at a distance. A second way is to find a company that offers visitors the chance to enter a shark cage that is lowered into the ocean. This allows a barrier between humans and sharks. The final excursion type takes groups of experienced divers beneath the ocean to actually swim with hammerheads. While this may seem dangerous, following some rules minimizes the chance of danger.

Divers swim unharmed with hammerhead sharks.

Following these rules can help make an in-person encounter with a hammerhead safe for both you and the shark:

Hammerhead sharks rarely attack people, but follow certain rules to stay safe.

1. **Never dive without an experienced guide.** These guides have had training and have the experience to recognize risky behaviors. Their job is to keep divers safe, but this can only be done if you follow their instructions. They are the ones who are leading the group for good reason.

2. **Wear black.** Blending into the shark's environment will help reduce the stress it feels. Bright colors may be mistaken for one of the colorful sea creatures it considers a snack. Many of the ocean's fish are brightly colored. When a shark sees a flash of color, its instinct is to chase after the color.

3. **Move slowly and never approach a shark.** In places where diving excursions often occur, the sharks are more comfortable around humans. One may approach you out of curiosity and may even bump you with its nose. If this happens, stay calm, and let it come to you rather than you approaching it. By moving towards the shark, you may activate its prey instinct, which could result in a reflex bite.

4. **Don't feed them.** While there are a few excursions that allow divers to feed sharks, this is done in a controlled manner. Feeding sharks that are not accustomed to it could result in a food-seeking swarm of hammerheads. Injuries may occur! Just stay close to the group and always follow directions.

5. **Don't corner a shark.** Remember, a shark that feels threatened is more likely to attack. Any animal, even a deer or a rabbit, will attack if it feels cornered. Make sure the hammerhead has a clear passage away from you. If given the chance, the shark will leave rather than fight, so give it that chance.

6. **Don't stay on the surface.** In the world of sharks, something that floats near the surface is either sick or dying, and this entices a shark to think of prey. You do not want to be aggressive toward the hammerhead, but you also do not want to appear weak. Making eye contact and not swimming too near the surface are both ways to appear less vulnerable.

7. **Learn the signs of stress.** A hammerhead will let you know when it is feeling stressed. Remember that they communicate with each other by body movements, and they will do the same with humans. Signs of stress include fast bursts forward, jerky movements resembling a dance, and an exaggerated side-to-side motion of its head (as if it's shaking its head no). Immediately stop doing whatever you are doing that's creating the stress, and give the shark room to escape.

8. **Don't dive at night.** Hammerheads do their hunting at night. You don't want to encounter a shark when it is hungry. It probably won't eat you, but it may take a bite to see if you are edible. Some tour boats make special trips at night, but most often, those taking the tour are required to stay in the boat and just observe the sharks from there.

9. **Show respect.** Remember, you are in the hammerhead's home. Show it the respect you would show to anyone you are visiting by learning the rules and following them. Some of the ways you can show respect are to learn what behaviors signal stress, give the shark enough personal space, and do not do anything that could cause it harm. Most of all, do not go into the situation thinking of sharks as vicious creatures. Allow your mind to put aside any stereotypes of sharks, and decide to give these beautiful creatures a chance.

RESEARCH PROJECTS

There are a few research projects that offer individuals a chance to join in when scientists tag hammerheads. Other projects look for individuals to help in the research facility. The best way to know what kinds of volunteer positions are available is to contact an individual facility and ask. In either case, you will be able to experience being near a hammerhead, and even touching one, in a safe environment.

There are a number of studies that use devices like tags or electronic monitoring equipment. These projects are interested in where a hammerhead travels and what its daily activities are like. These studies help scientists in two different ways. The data helps them understand the hammerhead's world, and it also helps them learn about the growth and decline of the hammerhead population. Researchers can find out things like where a group of hammerhead sharks relocates to when something makes it impossible for them to stay where they were. The information also helps scientists understand the impact of fishing, weather changes, and environmental accidents like pollution or oil spills.

AQUARIUMS

You won't find a great hammerhead shark in an aquarium because they are so large that they do not fare well in captivity. The hammerhead shows an increased negative response to stress when it is captured. This is greater than in any other species of shark. Smaller hammerheads can be kept in aquariums where the space is large enough to help hammerheads feel safe. Visiting an aquarium will allow you to see hammerheads in person without any danger involved because a pane of glass separates the two of you. In the future, aquariums may not exist because more people are learning that wild animals do not survive well in captivity. Someday, laws may prevent aquariums from keeping any wild animal captive.

Smaller hammerhead sharks can be found in aquariums.

SEEK A RELATED CAREER

People who think they may enjoy working with sharks as a career for the rest of their lives have several opportunities. Most of these careers involve knowing a lot about science, but there are others that do not require as much. Here are some ideas to explore:

1. Oceanographer – A person who studies all areas of ocean life.

2. Researcher – A person who works with different groups in a variety of positions, typically discovering or verifying information.

3. Tour Guide – Someone who takes divers out to experience swimming among sharks.

4. Conservationist – Someone who works to make sure the population of a certain plant or animal stays safe.

5. Veterinarian – These are animal doctors. Some veterinarians work in aquariums and with research groups to help take care of ill sharks.

SIDEBAR

FINAL THOUGHTS

Hammerhead sharks are among the most amazing members of the shark world. These animals simply want to live their lives the way that they and their ancestors have always lived. As the human population takes over more and more of their coastal territories, they have tried to adapt. It is not always possible for them to avoid human contact entirely. They are willing to live in peace with humans as long as they feel safe. As humans, we have the ability to learn about how they think and act naturally. This makes it easier for us to coexist with them peacefully. All it takes is a willingness to see the hammerhead as the special creature it is, and respect its right to live as a shark, not what a human thinks a shark should be.

INFORMATION DISPLAYS

There are places that set up interactive displays to help teach people about ocean life and other environments. Visiting one of these events will allow you to do things such as view videos, read about hammerheads, and listen to lectures with many different types of information regarding the shark's life.

You probably won't see a live hammerhead at one of these displays, but you may see one that has died and been preserved. In other cases, you may see a life-sized model.

ACCIDENTAL ENCOUNTERS

All of the above are encounters that you choose to make with the hammerhead,

Some artists include the hammerhead shark in their paintings—such as this graffiti artist in Melbourne, Australia.

but what should you do if you are out in a boat or swimming and encounter one? While nobody can guarantee a safe ending to such an encounter, keep in mind that the hammerhead is one of the most docile of sharks and is not likely to attack unless it feels trapped or threatened. Some exceptions to this may be if the shark has been injured, or you happen to come across one that has been fleeing a stressful encounter. There are things you can do to reduce the risk of an actual attack.

1. **Don't panic.** One of the worst things you can do is panic. This will cause you to make loud noises and react with quick motions that can be misinterpreted as an attack. Try to stay calm. This may not be easy because a person's natural instinct is to feel scared when they see a shark in the water. Try to remember that most sharks would rather be left alone without any kind of trouble.

2. **Stay still.** This is especially true if you're in a boat. The hammerhead may simply be curious, and by staying still, you allow it to satisfy its curiosity without feeling threatened. If you move around wildly and yell loudly, the shark will feel like it may be in danger and will want to defend itself.

3. **Move slowly and quietly.** If staying still isn't an option, move as slowly and quietly as possible in order to keep the shark feeling calm. If possible, keep looking at its eyes. Knowing you see it and are on guard will make it think twice about causing trouble.

4. **Get out of the water.** If you are swimming, move quickly but quietly toward the shore. The calmer you can remain, the less likely it is that you will upset the hammerhead, and chances are, it will simply go about its business and ignore you.

TEXT-DEPENDENT QUESTIONS:

1. What is the number one thing you should remember if you come into contact with a hammerhead unexpectedly?

2. What are the three ways you can see hammerheads on excursions?

3. Why won't you ever see a great hammerhead in captivity?

RESEARCH PROJECT:

Find information on a current hammerhead shark study, and write a paper on what the researchers are trying to learn. Make sure you include information on how the study is being conducted. End the paper with some ideas about what you would personally like to see the scientists research.

SERIES GLOSSARY OF KEY TERMS

Apparatus: A device or a collection of tools that are used for a specific purpose. A diving apparatus helps you breathe under water.

Barbaric: Something that is considered unrefined or uncivilized. The idea of killing sharks just for their fins can be seen as barbaric.

Buoyant: Having the ability to float. Not all sharks are buoyant. They need to swim to stay afloat.

Camouflage: To conceal or hide something. Sharks' coloring often helps camouflage them from their prey.

Chum: A collection of fish guts and fish remains thrown into the ocean to attract sharks. Divers will often use chum to help attract sharks.

Conservation: The act of preserving or keeping things safe. Conservation is important in keeping sharks and oceans safe from humans.

Decline: To slope down or to decrease in number. Shark populations are on the decline due to human activity.

Delicacy: Something, particularly something to eat, that is very special and rare. Shark fin soup is seen as a delicacy in some Asian countries, but it causes a decline in shark populations.

Expedition: A type of adventure that involves travel for a specific purpose. Traveling to a location specifically to see sharks would be considered an expedition.

Ferocious: Describes something that is mean, fierce, or extreme. Sharks often look ferocious because of their teeth and the way they attack their prey.

Finning: The act of cutting off the top (dorsal) fin of a shark specifically to sell for meat. Sharks cannot swim without all of their fins, so finning leads to a shark's death.

Frequent: To go somewhere often. Sharks tend to frequent places where there are lots of fish.

Ft.: An abbreviation for feet or foot, which is a unit of measurement. It is equal to 12 inches or about .3 meters.

Indigenous: Native to a place or region.

Intimidate: To scare or cause fear. Sharks can intimidate other fish and humans because of their fierce teeth.

Invincible: Unable to be beaten or killed. Sharks seem to be invincible, but some species are endangered.

KPH: An abbreviation for kilometers per hour, which is a metric unit of measurement for speed. One kilometer is equal to approximately .62 miles.

M: An abbreviation for meters, which is a metric unit of measurement for distance. One meter is equal to approximately 3.28 feet.

Mi.: An abbreviation for miles, which is a unit of measurement for distance. One mile is equal to approximately 1.61 kilometers.

Migrate: To move from one place to another. Sharks often migrate from cool to warm water for several different reasons.

MPH: An abbreviation for miles per hour, which is a unit of measurement for speed. One mile is equal to approximately 1.61 kilometers.

Phenomenon: Something that is unusual or amazing. Seeing sharks in the wild can be quite a phenomenon.

Prey: Animals that are hunted for food—either by humans or other animals. It can also mean the act of hunting.

Reputable: Something that is considered to be good or to have a good reputation. When diving with sharks, it is important to find a reputable company that has been in business for a long time.

Staple: Something that is important in a diet. Vegetables are staples in our diet, and fish is a staple in sharks' diets.

Strategy: A plan or method for achieving a goal. Different shark species have different hunting strategies.

Temperate: Something that is not too extreme such as water temperature. Temperate waters are not too cold or too hot.

Tentacles: Long arms on an animal that are used to move or sense objects. Octopi have tentacles that help them catch food.

Vulnerable: Something that is easily attacked. We don't think of sharks as being vulnerable, but they are when they're being hunted by humans.

INDEX

FURTHER READING

Benchley, Peter. *Shark Life: True Stories About Sharks & the Sea*. Yearling; Reprint edition (April 10, 2007). Learn about the real stories of sharks from a man who travelled the world to meet and study all the life that the oceans have to offer. These true stories are more exciting than any that could be made up.

Eilperin, Juliet. *Demon Fish: Travels Through the Hidden World of Sharks*. Anchor; Reprint edition (July 24, 2012). This book demonstrates how smart and often gentle sharks can be when treated correctly.

Helfman, Gene and George H. Burgess. *Sharks: The Animal Answer Guide*. Baltimore: Johns Hopkins University Press, 2014. In this book, you will find the answers to all the questions you have ever asked about sharks and some you never thought to ask.

Klimley, A. Peter. *The Biology of Sharks and Rays*. University of Chicago Press, 2013. This book takes you into what makes sharks unique among the animals that live beneath the water of our mysterious oceans.

Paragon Books. *Sharks* (Discovery Kids). Parragon Books (June 5, 2015). This book covers all manner of sharks, not just hammerheads.

INTERNET RESOURCES

https://www.youtube.com/results?search_query=SHARK+ACADEMY: Shark Academy uses videos to explore the world of many shark breeds.

http://cnso.nova.edu: The Halmos College of Natural Sciences and Oceanography provides shark videos and shark activity maps.

http://cnso.nova.edu/sharktracking: The Guy Harvey Research Institute (GHRI) Shark Tracking partners with the Halmos College of Natural Sciences and Oceanography in tracking and recording shark activity. The GHRI dedicates its resources to the preservation of marine life, including sharks.

http://saveourseas.com: The Save Our Seas Foundation focuses their efforts specifically on saving sharks and rays. Their website includes shark facts, a newsletter, and details about how to help save sharks and rays.

https://www.sharksider.com/: Sharksider covers a variety of shark information, offers a shark book for download, and offers a blog for updated shark information for those wanting to keep up on shark matters.

AT A GLANCE

SWIM DEPTH

— 200 ft.

Hammerhead Sharks
Length: 20 ft. (6.1 m)
Swim Depth: 262 ft. (80 m)
Lifespan: 20+ years

— 400 ft.

Bull Sharks
Length: 11.1 ft. (3.4 m)
Swim Depth: 492 ft. (150 m)
Lifespan: 18+ years

Rays
Length: 8.2 ft. (2.5 m)
Swim Depth: 656 ft. (200 m)
Lifespan: 30 years

— 600 ft.

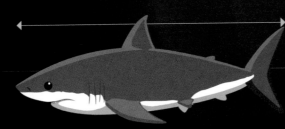

Great White Sharks
Length: 19.6 ft. (6 m)
Swim Depth: 820 ft. (250 m)
Lifespan: 30 years

— 800 ft.

Blue Sharks
Length: 12.5 ft. (3.8 m)
Swim Depth: 1,148 ft. (350 m)
Lifespan: 20 years

— 1,000 ft.

Tiger Sharks
Length: 11.5 ft. (3.5 m)
Swim Depth: 1148 ft. (350 m)
Lifespan: 50 years

— 1,200 ft.

Thresher Sharks
Length: 18.7 ft. (5.7 m)
Swim Depth: 1200 ft. (366 m)
Lifespan: 50 years

Mako Sharks
Length: 13.1 ft. (4 m)
Swim Depth: 1,640 ft. (500 m)
Lifespan: 32 years

— 1,400 ft.

— 1,600 ft.

Source: www.iucnredlist.org

— 1,800 ft.

PHOTO CREDITS

EDUCATIONAL VIDEO LINKS

Chapter 1
Watch hammerheads in action as they hunt! http://x-qr.net/1EDE

Chapter 2
This video shows the hammerhead and other sea life living inside the underwater volcano near Solomon Island: http://x-qr.net/1H9T

Chapter 3
Just how did the hammerhead develop its hammer? http://x-qr.net/1Cyx

Chapter 4
Tracking sharks: http://x-qr.net/1Fe4

AUTHOR'S BIOGRAPHY

Joyce has written nearly four thousand articles on a multitude of subjects. She is a published book author, has answered questions at AllExperts.com, and has ghostwritten articles for over twenty-five years. She uses her forensic psychology degree to aid in writing for many fields. These fields include psychology, criminology, sales, animal behavior, color psychology, education, and psychological disorders.